CW00540905

CREDIT REPAIR:

HOW TO REPAIR CREDIT WITH 609 DISPUTE LETTERS. BECOME A PRO AND RAISE YOUR SCORE QUICKLY WITH SECRETS STRATEGIES PROVEN IN 2020 (BOOK 2).

Tony Game

Table of Contents

Introduction

Getting yourself in the best possible financial shape is essential to your overall success in life. After all, without the right amount of money to support yourself and your family it's nearly impossible to do everything that you want and that's what life is all about. You want to be able to enjoy yourself as much as possible. But to truly live a happy life you need to make sure that you are financially stable and that means saving money, getting your credit in good shape and eliminating debt.

There are a variety of wrong ideas out there when it comes to credit scores. Some individuals have the belief that they have no credit score while some presume that the credit score is not all that essential. Having these kinds of misconceptions can hurt your finances and your life in general. Also, employers can utilize it in determining if a job with lots of responsibility is ideal for you, among a host of other things. By the time you finish reading, you will be armed with the needed information that will get you back in charge of your financial life.

Without good credit, you can't get that good job you need to earn enough money to pay your bills. Instead, you are forced to go to the highly expensive check cashing services, resort to ulterior means of getting the funds you need, or you're losing precious time away from family and friends so that you can get by and do what you need to do.

Credit is not just a matter of convenience, it is a way of life, and the more you struggle without it, the more you realize what you have lost.

The sad part is losing your credit means you've lost your good reputation in the community. People look at you differently, they respect you less, and they pull away when they know you don't have it. It is straightforward to lose your credit reputation, and yet many people have; in fact, millions have.

Many feel doomed to spend the rest of their lives, struggling to survive against all odds. It feels like everyone is against you no matter what you do. They are not interested in the person but are more focused on those numbers that claim to say all they can about you. This leads you to self-punishment, a sense of self-loathing in some cases, and feeling like you just don't want to try anymore.

Those with a low credit score are the ones that need the most help, and yet they are the ones that are less likely to get it. They don't search for help because society as a whole tells them they are not worthy, and few realize that something can be done about it.

If you're struggling with poor credit whether it is because of decisions on your part or something else, we will give you some tools to restore your right name and get you back on track. Most people struggle with a negative mark on their credit from time to time but don't be fooled into thinking there is no way back. Hopefully, by the time you finish reading this book, you'll be back on the road to a viable financial future with a more favorable financial image to give to the world.

By the time you finish reading, you will be armed with the needed information that will get you back in charge of your financial life. Here in this book is the answer you've been looking for. A chance to reclaim your life and provide you with everything you need to start again, on the right foot. When you have a bad credit rating, it can affect not only your ability to obtain a loan. It may also result in problems in terms of securing any type of credit. For instance, you may encounter problems when renting a property, paying deposits on your phone lines as well as other utilities, or getting a store financing. As such, it is necessary to pay attention to your credit rating. Should you find any inaccuracies or discrepancies in your credit report, you can carry out a credit repair by requesting, usually in writing, that the concerned credit bureau investigates the disputed items. In your request, you may include a supporting documentation, if available, or simply state your dispute and request for an investigation. If you haven't figured it out by now, everything in this world revolves around your credit score. Unfortunately, due to the current economic disaster, it is becoming more and more difficult for people in the US to obtain credit from the credit card companies, lenders, and big banks. This book was written with one purpose in mind, to show you how to manage and improve your already horrible credit score.

Getting yourself in the best possible financial shape is essential to your overall success in life. After all, without the right amount of money to support yourself and your family, it's nearly impossible to do everything that you want and that's what life is all about, right? You want to be able to enjoy yourself as much as possible.

Chapter 1
What Is Credit

C redit best serves those who don't need it. This is why credit is defined as being a game and I recommend that you learn how to play it. The moment you finally start to understand the power that proper credit can give you; you should see things my way. Most of us only know the feeling of having the world on our shoulders because of our financial struggles, we get stuck on the bill paying treadmill. Our money is accounted for before we even get it in our possession. Waking up in the morning can be hard when you don't see a way out, having a dead end job, no job or just being broke can discourage anyone and force them to become content with the options they are given. Bad credit can make you feel like you are not living up to your full potential. It does not feel right cutting corners and always having to find an alternative way when it comes to anything related to using your name and credit. I know this is the reality of a lot of people reading this, but it does not have to stay this way.

Knowing you possess the ability and having a chance to take advantage of opportunities will make it a little easier to get out of bed in the morning, but first you must learn how. I am not here to give you a motivational speech or sell you dreams; I am here to let you know that we are all capable of doing so much more than we think we can regardless of the position we are in today. Only if we had more help, if only we had more money, if only we could be in position to take advantage of individual opportunities that come our way. We all have these types of conversations in our head, but what will you do about it?

Learning about credit and finance can be an intimidating task, I believe one should seek to understand anything they choose to participate in, and to be honest, we don't have a choice when it comes to credit. Knowledge is beautiful, but applied knowledge is compelling, the worse feeling in the world is to feel helpless, hopeless, or ignorant about anything, especially within a system that others are benefitting from while you are just forced through the motions. Why not have the knowledge and understanding of credit regardless of any trade or career you are in or will pursue credit can always be used as a tool of leverage no matter how much money you have or make. Pay attention to how even the wealthy people secure mortgages to purchase their property and pay interest while still building equity.

What is credit?

It's simple, credit is your credibility as related to your name and social security number; your credibility is built from your financial borrowing patterns. You can develop creditability with any nation, organization, company, or individual, but being financially credible, as we know it here in America comes from our dealings with lenders, banks, and other forms of financial institutions. These financial entities furnish our information to credit agencies and companies that import then summarized our activities into algorithms, which they use to generate credit scores. These credit agencies also referred to as credit bureaus are corporations that store our information in a file to identify our past and current creditability but more importantly, they determine our future credit worthiness. Your past behavior will dictate your current credit standing, if you can be trusted to borrow a small sum, pay it back on set terms, you will then become more credible. It's that simple.

If you let a friend of yours borrow $50 and they couldn't or wouldn't pay you back, would you trust them to borrow $5,000 after they failed to pay back the first loan? The common sense answer would be no if you are thinking from a business perspective, lenders are in business to earn money from interest from borrowers like you and me, and they do not want to gamble. Good credit when appropriately built and over time can open up possibilities of you walking into an institution, borrowing millions of unsecured dollars and be trusted actually to pay the balance back, it's that powerful. Of course you will need a strategy, sometimes collateral, but most importantly the ability to service the debt.

What determines if you have good credit?

35% OF YOU SCORE IS YOUR PREVIOUS PAYMENT HISTORY- You need a track record, trust comes with time just as you wouldn't fully trust a stranger on the street; don't expect for creditors to trust you unless you have proven yourself over time with your actions.

30% OF YOUR SCORE IS THE AMOUNT OF DEBT YOU CARRY with HOW MUCH CREDIT IS AVAILABLE - Just because you can, doesn't mean you should. If you start with a credit card that has a limit of $500, you don't want to carry a balance of more than $150. If you carry balances of more than 30% of your overall available credit, your score will suffer. So think about it, the more credit you have available the less your score is affected by carrying higher balances. If you have $80,000 in combined credit card limits, and you carried a balance of $7,000, your credit score wouldn't be affected because your overall limits aren't close to being reached. Some might not trust themselves with that much credit, but its useful to have high credit card limits if you have a reason to carry balances from month to month. It's better to have it and don't need it, rather than need it and don't have it.

15% OF YOUR SCORE IS THE AVERAGE AGE OF YOUR ACCOUNTS- The longer your accounts are open and active, the better your score will be. As long as the account is positive reporting, I always advise people never to close old credit accounts or your credit scores will suffer, exceptions to this rule will be mentioned later. Do not open up new accounts just because you can without a strategy, the average

age of accounts will drop and make you seem to be a riskier borrower as each new account will lower that average.

10% OF YOUR SCORE IS THE MIXTURE OF CREDIT– You has many types of credit products that creditors will extend to you. Revolving credit is the most important to your score. It comes from credit cards that do not have a pre-set monthly payment, but a flexible monthly payment with a minimum payment determined by the balance that you carry that month. You charge nothing, and you pay nothing. Installment loans come from a predetermined amount borrowed by the consumer. Unlike a revolving line of credit, installment loans have the same monthly payment for a set amount of months determined before you receiving any funds or goods. Examples of terms might be, $200 a month for 12, 24, or 36 months. Even though a mortgage will be the most significant financial purchase in life for most people, favorable reporting mortgages are not as useful to credit building and our credit health as people might think.

10% OF YOUR SCORE IS NEW CREDIT AND INQUIRIES- Any time you apply for an account with a creditor and they pull your credit, it is documented and defined as a hard inquiry. The lenders who requested your credit report from a credit agency along with the date they pulled the report will all be on record as an inquiry on your credit file for 25 months. Allowing creditors to pull your credit multiple times will hurt your score, even if they don't approve you for any extension of credit. Checking your credit will not hurt your credit score.

Paying on time, keeping balances low and not applying for credit excessively will keep your credit in good health. There are many more factors that separate good credit from great credit, but I will present you the basics first. For those who want great credit instead of good credit, just keep reading as many other factors come into play and should be considered carefully. And of course I will teach you how to delete those negative accounts.

Chapter 2
Repair Credit Solution: General Notions

Basics of credit repair

By making your financial goals, setting your budget, finding ways to save money, and requesting a copy of your credit report, you've done your preliminary legwork in trying to get your finances back in order.

Now that all three credit reporting agencies have a copy of your credit report, it's time to roll up your sleeves and tackle the inaccurate information reported on your credit report.

Reviewing Your Credit Report

When you check each of your credit reports, whether it is on the website of the credit reporting agency where you can download it, or a hard copy of your report which you received in the mail, each entry must be accurately reported.

When you consider misleading or incorrect information on the credit report, the Equal Credit Reporting Act notes you have the right to dispute the submission with the credit reporting agency. The credit reporting agency has to re-examine the creditor's admission. The enquiry must be concluded within 30 days of receiving the lawsuit message.

If the borrower fails to respond within that period, the credit reporting agency must delete from the credit report the entry you are contesting. If the creditor replies and the inaccurate entry are corrected, the credit reporting agency will update your credit report. There is also the risk that the borrower can respond to the credit report and not make any changes in it. If you're not happy with your revised credit report, you should write a 100-word paragraph to clarify your side of the story on any of the remaining items on the credit report. This customer statement will then surface any time it appears on your credit report. If you don't want to write a 100-word paragraph on your credit report, you will be able to write another 120-day appeal letter from your most recent credit report.

When you access your credit report on the Website of the credit reporting agency, you will be able to dispute the incorrect entries online. The site will have boxes to check for inaccuracy alongside an appropriate reason. If you choose to write a personalized message, you can also use the same answers as appropriate. Sample answers would be:

- This is not my account.

- This was not late as indicated.

- This was not charged off.

- This was paid off in full as agreed.

- This was not a collection account.

- This is not my bankruptcy as indicated.

- This is not my tax lien as indicated.

- This is not my judgment as indicated.

What you shouldn't do:

- Alter your identity, or try to change it.

- The story is fictional.

• Check any information which is 100% correct.

What you should do:

• Read your emails, should you decide to send them to us. If a letter looks legitimate, credit reporting agencies will believe it has been written by a credit repair service, and they will not investigate the dispute.

• Use your original letterhead (if you do have one).

• Use the appeal form included with the credit report by the credit reporting agency, if you want.

• Provide some evidence suggesting the wrong entry is erroneous.

• Include the identification number for all communications listed on the credit report.

Common Credit Report Errors

Note, there could be various mistakes in each of the three credit reports. It is not uncommon to have positive coverage of an account on one article, but weak reports on another.

Here are some of the most common credit report errors.

• Listed wrong names, emails, or phone numbers.

• Data that refers to another of the same name.

• Duplicate details, whether positive or negative, about the same account.

• Records have negative, apparently positive information.

• Balances on accounts payable are still on view.

• Delinquent payment reports that were never billed in due time.

• This indicates wrong credit limits.

• Claims included in the insolvency which are still due.

• Incorrect activity dates;

• Past-due payments not payable.

• Court records which are falsely connected with you, such as convictions and bankruptcy.

• Tax liens not yours.

• Unprecedented foreclosures.

Spotting Possible Identity Theft

Checking your credit report could also spot potential identity theft. That's why you should inquire at least once a year or every six months for a copy of your credit report.

Things to look for would be:

- Names of accounts and figures that you do not know.

- You don't remember filling out loan applications.

- Addresses you didn't live in.

- Poor bosses or tenants enquiries you don't know.

Creditors Can Help

Many times, if you have had a long-term account with a creditor, you can contact them directly and explain the error being reported on your credit report.

Ask them to write you a letter with the email and correction. Also ask them to contact every credit reporting agency that reports this incorrect entry to correct.

Once the creditor receives a copy of the letter, make a copy of it and attach the letter to the letter of dispute you send. Mail it to the agency for credit reporting, and ask them to update their files. Once that is completed, you will be sent back a new credit report by the credit reporting agency.

Credit Rescoring

Rapid rescoring is an expedited way of fixing anomalies in the credit file of a customer. The bad news is, you can't do it yourself. A fast rescore dispute process works through borrowers and mortgage brokers, many approved registry credit reporting companies, and credit reporting agencies.

If you are a creditor applying for a rescore on your credit report, you would need to provide detailed documents that would be sent to the collateral agencies that are working on your case. Cash registry is the system used by cash grantors. The data archive gathers the records from the three central credit reporting agencies. It has to check the consumer's initial information for a rescore. Once the verification is entered into the program of the repository a new score will be produced.

The critical thing to keep in mind is that a simple rescore can only be temporary. You may be able to close a loan with it. Still, you must follow through on your credit report with the three leading credit reporting firms to ensure it has been removed or corrected. If it reappears, forward the reports immediately to credit reporting agencies.

The downside of a fast rescore is that you save money without having to contend individually with a credit reporting agency that may take longer than 30 days to complete an audit. If the sale of a house or lease depends on your credit score, and you're in a time crunch, the best solution is to rescore easily.

Should You Use a Credit Repair Company?

Using a credit repair company's services is hiring a firm to do what you can do for yourself. The process is really without secrets. All the credit repair company does is dispute information on negative entries on your credit report with credit reporting agencies. Most companies may report having agreements with credit reporting agencies or have a secret way to get borrowers to delete unfavorable entries. This is more than likely not true because both state and federal laws under the Fair Credit Reporting Act regulate the credit reporting agencies.

You will be charged a fee for working with a credit repair company. Many systems will call up your credit records or allow you to access your reports. The letter-writing campaign starts after you have entered into a contract with the firm.

The reason some people hire an outsourced credit repair company is because they feel intimidated or have no time to do the work themselves. Until signing up with a credit repair company there are many steps you need to take. Many businesses operate illegally and you don't want to get caught in that trap.

Beware of Credit Repair Scams

Sadly, it is easy for people to fall prey to credit repair fraud when they are vulnerable and are going through financial challenges. If you're looking for a repair company for cash, here's how to say if it's a legitimate or scam business. Many scam firms may only sign up to take the money and run for their services. This is a list of stuff that should raise a red flag.

The company wants you to pay for credit repair services before it provides any services.

•   The company doesn't tell you your rights, and you can do it for free. This should appear in any document it presents you with.

•   The firm advises that you do not explicitly approach any of the three major national credit reporting agencies. It knows that if you do, you may learn that it took your money, and that it does nothing.

•   The company tells you that even if that information is accurate, it can get rid of all the adverse credit reports in your credit report. No one can promise just one thing on your credit report for change.

•   The company assumes you're trying to create a "different" credit identifier. This is known as file segregation. It is accomplished by filing for the use of an Employer Identification Number to create a new credit report instead of the Social Security number. That is utterly unconstitutional.

• The firm encourages you to challenge any information contained in your credit report regardless of accuracy or timeliness of the material. If the evidence is 100% right, then you have no basis for a disagreement.

Remember, if you are given unlawful advice and follow it knowing it is illegal, you may be committing fraud, and you will find yourself in lawful hot water.

If you use the postal, mobile, or Internet to apply for credit and provide false information, you could be charged and prosecuted with mail or wire fraud. Most of the programs you sign on have a promise that the details you receive are valid when signing the contract.

The Credit Service Organizations Act

Credit repair facilities are governed under State and Federal law by the Credit Service Organizations Act. Under this act, most states require that credit repair companies in each state where they do business be registered and bonded. There are different requirements for each Country. When signing up for this program you will check a copy of your state's Credit Service Organizations Act. The Federal Trade Commission and the offices of the State Attorney General are going after credit repair companies that do not comply with the regulations and are soliciting customers with misleading information. Through visiting: www.ftc.gov, you can also get a copy of the state edition of the Credit Service Organizations Act.

Some of this law's key provisions are for consumer protection by signing up with a credit repair service. A credit repair company must give you a written contract that outlines your rights and obligations that its state has approved. Make sure to read the paperwork before signing something. So know that a credit repair company can't:

•   Make false claims about its facilities, before signing.

•   Charge yourself until the promised services are complete.

•   Provide certain activities until a formal contract has been signed and a three-day waiting period has been fulfilled. You will cancel the contract during this period, without paying any fees.

Chapter 3
How to Pay Down Debt

Remember that you need to focus on paying off all your debts at the earliest. You cannot waste any more time and must try and finish them off to have a good score. Let us now look at the things that you need to do to pay off your debts on time.

You can pay off your debts in one of the two methods that are made available viz. the first one being the avalanche method and the second being the snowball method. Each type has its advantages and disadvantages. You need to look at whatever fits your budget best and go for it without wasting any more time. If you think you have enough money saved up then choose the avalanche method but if you have very little then chose the snowballing method. Apart from these, if you have enough money to pay everything all together then you can choose that option as well.

Planning

Remember to always work with a plan. When you have everything planned out it will be easy for you to finish your task. Start by preparing a monthly budget by including your incomes and expenses and try and balance it out to remain with as much money at the end as possible. You need to add your debts to the expenses column and this will help you pay them on time. When you are left with a surplus, you can use it to open a separate "debt repayment" account and add in the money there. Once you have a substantial amount, you can use it to pay off all your debts.

Organizing

Little planning will not suffice and you need to be as organized as possible. You must have everything in place to help you operate smoothly. Try having a different account for each of your debts so that money automatically gets transferred every month. You must also have a set monthly budget for your expenses. You must not use any more money than what you have assigned. When you are organized, you will feel that your life is easy and there are not many obstacles standing in your way.

Contact

The next step is to contact your creditors. This means that you get in touch with them and assure them that you are going to pay your debts on time. Many times, it pays to develop a good rapport with your creditors. But don't push it and remain within your limits. You need to develop a rapport and not a close friendship with them. You need to win over their trust and make them like your determination. Remain in touch with them and update them on your every move to repay their debts on time. After a while, the informality between the two of you will start to reduce.

Negotiate

When you have struck a good rapport, you can decide to ask for a small rebate in your debt or negotiate the rate of interest that you have to pay. This might not be possible with all creditors such as banks. Still, you can try your luck with moneylenders and other non-commercial lenders. Once they are happy with your timely debt repayments they might decide to reduce the interest rate by a little. But don't expect them to waive off your loan as nobody will be willing to do that. You can ask them if you can pay a little less for the last few installments and count that as your rebate.

Secured credit card

When you are trying to pay off all your debts at the earliest, you must not use your credit card excessively. Your credit score will plummet and so, you should give up on these. There are alternatives to credit cards that you can consider. Debit cards are a great idea as you will only draw money from your account when you use these. Buy if you want to have the feel of a credit card then you can opt for a secured credit card. These are issued by your bank and they will be linked to your account. You will have to add money to this account and there will be a limit on how much you can draw in a month. There will be no interest levied on the amount and you must add back the money that you withdrew within a specified time to help the account remain active.

Family

Sometimes, if there is a lot of debt then you can consider borrowing some money from your relatives. When you do so, you will be able to pay off a debt quickly. Your family members might not charge you a high rate of interest and it might be within your budget. You can consider asking your dad or your uncle or anybody who is in a position to pay you the amount at the earliest. You need not stress over paying the sum back to them and can do it leisurely and at your own pace.

Life insurance

It is also possible for you to borrow money from your life insurance policy. You can ask for a certain amount that you promise to pay back within a specified time. Once approved, you can use the money to pay off your debts or at least a majority of it. There is no interest as such that will be levied on this sum and you can repay it after a few years. Once you repay your debt and give back to your insurance company then you will indeed be free and your credit score will start to rise high.

Bank borrowing

It pays to have everything unified to make for secure payments. This means that you can borrow a certain amount from your bank and pay off all your creditors in bulk. You can then pay only to your bank to settle your debts. This will make it easier for you as you have to pay to only one institution. The rate of interest might also be low and that will help you save on a lot of money. The only disadvantage of this type is that, not many banks entertain this sort of borrowing. However, you can try your luck and approach two or more banks with a proposal.

Money savers

Every month, think of ways in which you can save on money. This can be by way of using coupons while shopping or making use of store credit to help save on the bill etc. You can also sell your old and unused stuff to make some money out of it. It is also a good idea to gift a service instead of a physical gift as this will further help you in saving money. Nevertheless, if you cannot gift a service every time then you can consider buying them in bulk after the holiday is over and store it to be gifted the next year. Cutting down on electricity, water and gas bills will also help you save money. It is also ideal for you to buy second hand goods for the time being and save further.

You can follow these steps to repay all your loans at the earliest and improve your credit score.

Chapter 4
Why Is My Credit Score Harming?

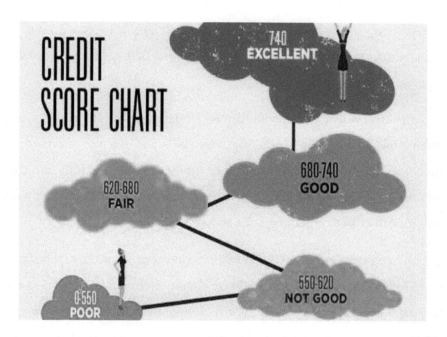

N ow that we have taken some time to look at the different things that are going to raise your credit score, we also need to take a closer look at some of the different parts that are going to end up harming the credit scores that we have. If you are in the process of fixing your credit, you want to make sure that you are careful and that you are not going to end up doing something that will harm your credit in the process. Some of the different things that we can watch out for when it comes to harming your credit score include:

Paying Late or Not at All

One of the worst things that you can do when it comes to your credit score is paying late on anything. About 35 percent of your score is going to be about your history of making payments or not on time. Consistently being late on these payments is going to cause a lot of damage to your credit score. Always pay your bills on time, especially your credit card bills.

What is even worse than paying late is not paying at all. If you decide to completely ignore your cards and other bills and not pay them at all, then you are going to be in even more trouble as well. Each month that you miss a payment for your credit card, you are going to end up with one month closer to helping your account be charged off.

If you ever want a chance to get your credit score up at all, especially if you are hoping to get it up to 800 or higher, then you have to stop the late payments. This is going to be a bad thing because it shows that you are not willing to pay your money back, and they are less likely to give you some more money in the process.

Having an Account Charged Off or Sent to Collections

Next on the list is having your accounts charged off. When creditors are worried that you will never pay in your bills for loans or credit cards, they are going to use a process known as charging off your accounts. A charge off means that the insurer has pretty much given up on ever hearing from you again. This does not mean that you are no longer going to hold responsibility for this debt at all. This is one of the absolute worst things out there when it comes to your credit score.

One other issue is when one of your accounts is sent off to collections. Creditors are often going to work with debt collectors to work on collecting a payment out of you. Collectors could send your account to collections after, but sometimes before, charging it all off. This is never a good thing, no matter if the account is charged off at that time, either.

If you are to the point of your bills going to collections or being charged off, this means that you have not just missed one or two payments. It means that you have gone so long without paying the whole thing that the company figures they are never going to get it back. Either they have probably written it off as a tax break, or they have sold it to a credit collection company that will be bothering you a lot in the future.

Filing Bankruptcy

This is extreme that you should try to avoid at all costs. Bankruptcy is an extreme measure, and it is going to cause a lot of devastation to the score that you are working with. It is also going to be on your record for seven to ten years. It is a good idea to seek some alternatives, like working with counseling for consumer credit, before filing bankruptcy.

It is best if you can do everything that you can to avoid bankruptcy at all costs. It may seem like the best idea to work with. You assume that when you declare bankruptcy, you can just walk away from all of the debt that you have, and not have to worry about it ever again. This is not how this whole process is going to work for you at all, though.

Once the bankruptcy is complete, which is something that can take some time, then a new problem is going to occur. You have to then focus on how you will handle the black mark that is on your credit report for quite a bit of time. This could be anywhere from seven to ten years. And you can bet that creditors are not going to look all that kindly at that. You will find that it is almost impossible to get any kind of credit or any other monetary help that you need for a long time afterward.

And if you are not able to get on a budget and take control over your debts, you may get it all discharged. Still, then you are going to turn around, and before you know it, all of your money is gone again and you are facing bankruptcy again. This is never a good thing. You are not going to be offered the option of bankruptcy multiple times, and using this as a Band-Aid is not going to work.

To avoid bankruptcy, you need to go through and learn how to work with a budget and figure out the best ways to manage your money, no matter what the income is that you are working with. This is easier to manage than you may think and can help you to get on a reasonable payment schedule so that you can deal with your debts and get them paid off. The bankruptcy seems like an easy way to get out of the debt. Still, it haunts you for many years afterward, can make getting credit later on almost impossible, and it will not solve the underlying problem that got you to this situation.

High Balances or Maxed Out Cards

We always need to look at the balances that we are going to have on our credit cards all of the time. The second most important part that comes with our credit score is the amount of debt that is on them, and that is going to be measured out by credit utilization. Having high balances for credit cards, relative to the credit limit that you are working with, will increase the utilization of credit and will make your credit score goes down. For example, if you have a limit of $10,000 on a card, but the balance is at $9500 or higher, then your score is not going to reflect positively with this one.

We also need to make sure that we are not maxing out or going over the limit when it comes to our credit cards. Credit cards that are over the limit or that have been maxed out are going to make the credit utilization that you have at 100 percent. This is going to be one of the most damaging things that you can do with your credit score. Make sure to pay down those debts as fast as you can to maintain your credit score and keep it from going over the top.

Closing Credit Cards

There are a few ways that closing your card is going to end up with a decrease in your credit score. First, we need to look at closing up a card that still has a balance on it. When you close that card, the credit limit you get to work with is going to end up at $0, while your balance is still going to be the same. This is going to make it look like you have been able to max out the credit card, which is going to cause your score to drop a bit. If you want to close your account, then you need to make sure that you pay off the balance before you close it.

Another thing to consider is what will happen when you close out your old credit cards. About 15 percent of your credit score is going to be the length of your credit history, and longer credit histories are going to be better. Closing up old cards, especially some of the oldest cards are going to make your history seem like it is a lot shorter than it is. Even if you do not use the card anymore, and there are no annual fees, and you should keep the card open because you are losing nothing and gaining more.

Not Having Enough Mix on the Report

While this is not as big of a deal as some of the other options, you will find that having a good mix of credit is going to be about 10 percent of your credit score at the time. If you have a report that only has one or two things on it, such as either credit cards or loans, then it is likely the score you are working with will be affected in some way or another.

The more that you can mix up your accounts and get them to have many different things on them, the better. You don't want to overextend yourself, but having a mix of loans, mortgage, credit cards, and more, that you pay off each month without fail, is going to be one of the best ways that you can raise your credit score without causing harm or paying too much in the process.

This does not mean that you should go out and apply for a bunch of different things all at once to get your mix up. This is something that often happens; naturally, the longer you work on your credit score. You may have a few credit cards. And then you take out a loan for a car and pay it off. Maybe you need a loan for a vacation or some home improvement so you will have those accounts. And then get a mortgage too.

Applying for Too Much

Another thing that is going to count on your report is the credit inquiries. These will take up about 10 percent of the score that you work with. Making several applications for loans and credit in a short amount of time is going to cause a big drop in your credit score along the way. Always keep the applications for credit to a minimum, so this doesn't end up harming you along the way.

In some cases, this is not going to harm you too much. For example, if you have a good credit score and you want to apply for a mortgage, you will want to apply for a few mortgages and shop around a bit. If you do these close together, then it is not going to be seen as bad because the lender will assume this is what you are doing, rather than you taking on too much or that you have been turned down. You can also explain this to them easily if they ask.

These are just a few of the different things that we are going to work with when it comes time to handle our credit report. Sometimes the things that can harm your score are going to be much more important than the things that can help improve the score. Working on both is going to be important when it all comes down to it as well, and knowing how to avoid some of the common things that can ruin your credit in no time is imperative to getting that score up and seeing it work the way that you want.

Chapter 5
Section 609: What Is It?

What Is Section 609?

A609 is known as a dispute letter, which you would send to your creditor if you saw you were overcharged or unfairly charged. Most people use a 609 letter in order to get the information they feel they should have received. There are several reasons why some information might be kept from you.

A section 609 letter is sent after two main steps. First, you see that the dispute is on your credit report. Second, you have already filed and processed a debt validation letter. The basis of the letter is that you will use it in order to take unfair charges off your credit report, which will then increase your credit score.

The 609 letters can easily help you delete your bad credit. Other than this, there are a couple of other benefits you will receive from the letter. One of these benefits is that you will obtain your documentation and information as the credit bureau has to release this information to you. Secondly, you will be able to obtain an accurate credit report, which can definitely help you increase your credit score.

There are also disadvantages to the 609 letters. One of these disadvantages is that collection agencies can add information to your credit history at any time. A second disadvantage is that you still have to repay debt. You cannot use the 609 letters in order to remove debt that you are obligated to pay. Finally, your creditor can do their own investigation and add the information back into your credit report, even if it was removed (Irby, 2019).

One of the reasons section 609 came to be is because one of five people state they have inaccurate information on the credit report (Black, 2019). At the same time many people believe that this statistic is actually higher than 20 percent of Americans.

How Section 609 Works to Repair Bad Credit

If you notice anything on your report that should not be there, you need to use the section 609 loophole in order to file a dispute, which could result in their wrong information being taken off of the report.

If this is the case, your credit score will increase, as you will no longer have this negative inaccuracy affecting your score.

How to File a Dispute with Section 609

It is important to note that there are several template letters for section 609. What this means is that you can easily download and use one of these templates yourself. While you usually have to pay for them, there are some that are free. Of course, you will want to remember to include your information in the letter before you send it.

You will want to make sure everything is done correctly, as this will make it more likely that the information will come off and no one will place it back on your report again.

1. Find a dispute letter through Googling "section 609 dispute letters". While you might be able to find a free download, for some, you will be able to copy and paste into Microsoft Word or onto a Google Doc.

2. Make the necessary changes to the letter. This will include changing the name and address. You will also want to make sure your phone number is included. Sometimes people include their email address, but this is not necessary. In fact, it is always safer to only include your home address or PO Box information. You will also want to make sure to edit the whole letter. If something does not match up to what you want to say in your letter, such as what you are trying to dispute on your credit report, you need to state this. These letters are quite generic, which means you need to add in your own information.

3. You want to make sure that all of your account information you want to be taken off your credit report is handwritten. You also want to make sure you use blue ink rather than black. On top of this, you do not need to worry about being too neat, but you want to make sure they can read the letters and numbers correctly. This is an important part of filing your dispute letter because handwritten ones in blue ink will not be pushed through their automated system. They have an automatic system that will read the letter for them and punch in the account number you use. They will then send you a generic letter that states these accounts are now off your credit report, which does not mean that it actually happened. When you write the information down, a person needs to read it and will typically take care of it. Of course, this does not mean that you will not be pushed aside. Unfortunately, this can happen with any letters.

4. You want to make sure that you prove who you are with your letters. While this is never a comfortable thing to do, you must send a copy of your social security card and your driver's license or they will shred your letter. You also need to make sure that you get each of your letters notarized. You can typically do this by visiting your county's courthouse.

5. You can send as many letters as you need to; however, keep in mind that the creditor typically will not make you send more than four. This is because when you threaten to take them to court in the third letter, they will realize that your accounts and demands just are not worth it. First, you could damage their reputation, and secondly, you will cost

them more money than simply taking the information off your credit report will.

6. You will want to make sure that you keep all correspondence they send you. This will come in handy when they try to make you send more information or keep telling you that they cannot do anything. It is important that you do not give up. Many people struggle to get them to pay attention because that is just how the system works. Therefore, you need to make sure that you do not listen to their quick automatic reply that your information is off of your credit report. You also want to make sure to wait at least three months and then re-run your credit report to make sure the wrong information has been removed. Keep track of every time you need to re-run your credit report as you can use this as proof if they continue to send you a letter stating the information is off of your credit report.

It is important to note that you can now file a dispute letter online with all three credit bureaus. However, this is a new system, which means that it does come with more problems than sending one through the mail. While it is completely your choice whether you use a form to file your 609 dispute or send a letter, you always want to make sure you keep copies and continue to track them, even if you don't hear from the credit bureau after a couple of months. It will never hurt to send them a second letter or even a third.

What Are My Rights Under 609?

The Fair Credit Reporting Act is going to cover many of the aspects and the components of credit checking to make sure that it is able to maintain a reasonable amount of privacy and accuracy along the way. This agency is going to list all of the responsibilities that credit reporting companies and any credit bureaus will have, and it includes the rights of the consumer that will be your rights in this situation. This Act is going to be the part that will govern how everything is going to work to ensure that all parties are treated in a fair manner.

When using this act the consumer has to be told if any of the information that is on your file has been in the past or is now being used against you in any way, shape, or form. You have a right to know whether the information is harming you and what that information is.

In addition, the consumer is going to have the right to go through and dispute any information that may be seen as inaccurate or incomplete at the time. If they see that there are items in the documents they are sent, if the billing to them is not right or there is something else off in the process, the consumer has the right to dispute this and the credit reporting agency needs to at least look into it and determine if the consumer is right.

This Act is going to limit the access that third parties can have to your file. You personally have to go through and provide your consent before someone is able to go through and look at your credit score, whether it is a potential employer or another institution providing you with funding.

They are not able to get in and just look at it. Keep in mind that if you do not agree for them to take a look at the information, it is going to likely result in you not getting the funding that you want, because there are very few ways that the institution can fairly assess the risk that you pose to them in terms of creditworthiness.

It means that you may have debt or another negative item that is on your credit report, but there is a way to get around this without having to wait for years to get that to drop off your report or having to pay back a debt that you are not able to afford.

Keep in mind that this is not meant to be a method for you to take on a lot of debts that you cannot afford and then just dump them. But on occasion, there could be a few that you are able to fight and get an instant boost to your credit score in the process.

Why Use a 609 Letter?

The 609 Letter is going to be one of the newest credit repair secrets that will help you to remove a lot of information on your credit report, all of the false information and sometimes even the accurate information, thanks to a little loophole that is found in our credit reporting laws. You can use this kind of letter in order to resolve some of the inaccuracies that show up, to dispute your errors, and handle some of the other items that could inaccurately come in and impact and lower your credit score.

Using these 609 letters is a good way for us to clean up our credit a bit and in some cases; it is going to make a perfect situation. However, we have to remember that outside of some of the obvious benefits that we are going to discuss, there are a few things that we need to be aware of ahead of time.

There are few limitations that are going to come with this as well, for example, even after you work with the 609 letters, it is possible that information that is seen as accurate could be added to the report again, even after the removal. This is going to happen if the creditor is able to verify the accuracy. They may take it off for a bit if the 30 days have passed and they are not able to verify at that point. But if the information is accurate, remember that it could end up back on the report.

Chapter 6
What Do I Need To Include
In My Dispute?

I t is important to gain as much information as possible so you can write the best letter. While you might not care to do this when it comes to the credit bureau, they often pay more attention to letters that are done professionally. Furthermore, many letters are placed to the side because the customer did not include all the information or correct documentation.

This will help you ensure that your letter is the best it can be before you send it to the credit bureau. These are not only tips detailing the information you should put into your dispute letter, but they are also tips from people who have successfully used the 609 loopholes to repair their credit.

Include Documentation

When it comes to your dispute letter, it is important to remember that documentation is key. Two factors go into making sure you provide proof. First, this makes your case that what is written on your credit report is wrong. Even though the credit bureau still has up to 90 days to investigate your claims, making sure to send documentation is going to result in your case being even stronger. Furthermore, it proves that you completely understand what this wrong information is doing to your credit report and that you intend to fix this, which your right is provided by section 609.

You want to include as much documentation as you need to. This means that you can send a copy of your credit report, including highlighting the information that it wrong. At the same time, you need to make sure that the information is also handwritten in your letter. Enclosing a copy of your credit reports simply proves that this information is truly on your report and it is not made up.

You also want to make sure that you include the information to verify that you really are yourself. If copies of your identification card, such as a state-issued ID or driver's license along with your social security card are not enclosed, they might not take any action with your letter. The fact is that this letter could have been written and sent by anyone.

You also want to make sure that you send any copies of checks, credit card receipts, and any correspondence. This means that if you are sending your second letter to the credit bureau, you should also include your first letter.

Never send originals to the credit bureau. You always want to make sure that you send copies and keep the originals for yourself.

Be Thorough

You want to make sure you are concise with your information but also thorough. This might mean that you spend a good amount of time writing your letter. It is important that you keep it about a page in length, make sure that everything is readable, and you don't make the print to small. The best font to use is Times New Roman and the best size to use is 12-point font. This is standard when it comes to business letters. You don't need to pick the fun font as this is not meant to be a fun and interesting letter; it is meant to be straight to the point and to provide all the information necessary.

The trick is to simply state the facts, such as what is wrong and what you want to happen so the issue is resolved. You don't really need to explain why you think it is wrong, but you need to explain what the situation is. Explaining the whys will make the letter too long. Furthermore, this isn't the information that the credit bureau wants to see in the letter, as they don't care about the why.

Illustrate Your Case

You want to make sure that you explain what about the information you believe to be wrong. You don't just want to say that certain information on your credit report is wrong and you would like it removed and then list the incorrect information. You want to make sure that you give them information that makes you prove it is wrong in a written way. For example, you can state that you know you made credit card payments to Capital One during the months of June and July in 2018. You will want to give them the numbers for the incorrect information, which will be shown on your credit report, and then move on to the next item or finish the letter. You will then want to include documentation proving that you made these payments.

Proofread the Letter Thoroughly

You don't want to be in so much of a hurry to send this letter that you spell something incorrectly. This is going to reflect negatively on you. Even though misspellings happen, this short and simple letter won't take longer than a few minutes to edit.

It is important not just to read the words but also to make sure all the numbers are correct. It is common for people to mix up a couple of digits when there is a long series of numbers. Therefore, take an extra minute or two to make sure that every number matches up to your credit report.

Proofreading your letter will also help you make sure that you have all the necessary information but did not become too detailed. If you don't feel comfortable proofreading your own letter, take it to a friend or family member to look at it.

You can also match up your information with the templates online to make sure you have everything that you need in the letter.

Get Advice If Necessary

If you want to make sure that you are reading your credit report correctly or you want to get reassurance that you are correct, you can seek advice from a professional. You don't have to contact an attorney; you can simply go to your financial advisor or someone else you trust for help. For example, loan advisors at banks regularly read credit reports and might be willing to help you, especially if you have a relationship with the banker.

Of course, there is also a lot of advice that you can find online. There are a lot of people who share their stories of writing letters and are willing to help you with anything you need to make sure that you get all incorrect information taken off your report.

What Not to Disclose in Your Letter

It is just as important to make sure that you don't disclose certain information.

First, you never want to disclose what you don't want to dispute. This means that you don't want to place anything in your letter that is correctly on your credit report. Some people will often scan their credit report and black out the other information that the credit bureau does not need to see with the letter. They might do this in order to highlight what is wrong or for their own protection.

Secondly, unless you have a legitimate reason to do so and you have gotten advice from an attorney, you do not want to threaten legal action. This can be okay to do by the time you are sending your third letter. However, you always want to make sure to get legal advice before you threaten to sue anyone. This is just an extra step to make sure that you do not cross any legal lines that you are unaware of.

Third, you don't want to dispute any credit card payments that you fell behind on recently. There is a statute of limitations, which means that if you did not make the last two payments on a credit card that states you didn't make two payments last year, when you know you did, leave this dispute out. Because you are currently behind, this will reflect negatively on you and it can have your whole case thrown out.

Finally, there are ways that you can dispute over the phone or online. However, it is advised that you never do this. One of the main reasons you don't want to do this is you are not allowed to keep copies of correspondence. While you never want to end up going to court over this claim, and it is rare that this happens, you always want to act like this could happen. Another reason is that when you try to dispute over the phone, you need to agree to certain terms verbally. These are often stated in a very confusing way. One of the most common agreements made over the phone that you would never agree to on paper is to waive any right to a reinvestigation. This means that if the credit bureau states nothing could be found to support your claim, you cannot try to reopen the case. In general, disputing online or over the phone is a huge disadvantage for you.

Make Sure Everything Is Readable

No matter what you send, you want to make sure that someone else will be able to read it. This is another reason why having someone proofread your letter is often the best option as they will be able to tell you if something isn't readable or doesn't make sense.

While you should do your best to type as much information as possible, you shouldn't write the letter by hand. While this will be accepted, it is generally not something that people do in this day and age. Furthermore, typing most of the information will ensure that words are not mistaken for another word, which can happen with handwriting.

While you might feel your handwriting is easily readable, someone else might not be able to understand it as well.

Don't Bypass the Credit Reporting Agency

Some people feel that having to write a dispute letter to the credit bureau is the long road. Instead, they want to direct it to the lender. This is a common mistake that people make and one that can make the process longer than it initially is.

Another reason people often go directly to the lender is that section 609 states that you can do this. However, this also makes it so you have more difficulty fighting your case. Chances are that the lender is not going to fix the mistake very easily. If you find that you need to take stronger measures, you could have a bigger struggle on your hands because you did not contact the credit bureau first.

Chapter 7
Procedure for Making Letters of Dispute

Writing the Dispute Letter

Removing adverse information from your credit report is the most vital step when trying to improve your score on a short-term basis.

Credit reporting agencies (CRAs) are not obligated to give notification when adverse information is being reported about you. Upon receiving your information, the CRAs' only job under the law is to use their "reasonable procedures" to validate accuracy.

However, there is no proper and detailed explanation of these procedures, like a list of what must be performed. Of course, if the

CRAs were legally required to corroborate every piece of information they receive, they will burn out and shut down.

The Disputing Process

The first thing you need to know is that all three credit reporting agencies have to contest the inaccurate information independently. The disputed appearance may be on all three credit reports, or may not. Keep in mind that customers may not belong to all credit reporting agencies. This is why you will see that on one list some of the investors are not on the others.

Even though all three credit reporting agencies have the same information, this does not mean that if an item comes out of one credit report it will come out of the others. No promise is provided what the outcome will be. That is why you have to refute any inaccurate information about each particular article.

They can use their appeal forms when disputing with credit reporting agencies, write your own message, or challenge the item online on their Website. If you decide to dispute by letter writing, simply state the facts in a simple, concise or two sentences.

If you've found more than four entries on your credit report that you need to dispute, don't dispute everything in one letter. Whether you're writing a letter, filling out their form or answering via the Internet, break your disputes. You send or go back every 30 days to the website of the credit reporting agency, and challenge up to four more things. Don't overshoot that number. If you have to challenge less than four things, go ahead and dispute the remaining entries. Extend the spacing of conflicts for 30 days.

On submitting each address, expect to receive a revised credit report about 45 days after you send your letter or disagreement online. If your new credit report has not been issued before it's time to appeal the second time, go ahead and mail your second letter or challenge online instead.

Once all the grievance letters have been mailed or posted to their website and all the revised credit reports have been received, check whether products have been omitted or incomplete. If you need to do the procedure again for the remaining items, space 120 days from your most recent update to the next round of disputes.

CRAs Verification Forms

The FCRA tries to balance the game for consumers with the dispute process.

The dispute process gave the CRAs so much work, so they opted to restructure their dispute process—so they designed and provided a dispute form for consumers and separate verification forms for their source creditors.

Unsurprisingly, completing and returning verification forms are easier for creditors. Moreover, because the CRAs have 30 days to answer to your dispute, either to verify or correct an item, creditors are given a few weeks to return the CRAs the verification forms. However, bear something in mind: not every source creditor will turn around these forms within the allotted period—some will not even return it, at all. Just because of this, several disputes will bring about items being corrected or deleted.

Fill-In Dispute Forms

Below is an example of a multiple choice dispute options:

[ ] The account/item is not mine.

[ ] The account status is incorrect.

[ ] The account/item is too old to be included in my report.

When trying to initiate a dispute using the online platform, a pop-up may come to ask you if you want to dispute an item. Just select "yes" to continue.

This is just a protection clause used by the CRAs to trick you into thinking that it is illegal to dispute an item the CRAs consider as valid or correct.

Scale through their scare tactic and do not be intimidated. Just know that it is under the law for you to dispute any inaccurate information or item.

If you requested for your reports to be sent via email, among the documents will be a dispute form. The CRAs will advise to fill this already typed form only if there are any inaccuracies on your report. The funny thing is that these mailed dispute forms are simpler to complete because of two reasons: 1) Broadcasting their conformity to the legally required dispute process gives them more acclaim.

2) Supplying their forms is more convenient for them—because, with these simplified forms, their trained agents can swiftly read and convey the information on to their creditor verification forms.

If you have simple disputes (listed in a box or a line on the form), you can either use the online or mailed disputes forms. However, if your issues are complex or lengthy and cannot fit into the allotted space or there are not enough options on the document to address all your dispute issues, you may need to write the CRAs.

Concerning the mailed fill-in dispute forms, be cautious when filling them out as they may ask you to give out more personal information to the CRAs than you need to. The CRAs asking for more information does not mean you have to provide it. Just remember that if a fill-in dispute form does not adequately help your case, the best course of action is to write your letter.

How to write your Own Dispute

Letter

After organizing all your items, you can write your letter, but make sure to put your disputes in one correspondence. It does not matter if you have a long list of disputes. You can arrange your disputes on multiple pages and in different ways.

For instance, in the left column, list all your accounts; in the right column, list the issues in a few words ("not my account," "always paid on time/never late," etc.). Alternatively, you explain your dispute first, then list the accounts associated with the issue. For example, "the following accounts do not belong to me. . ." Just keep it short and straightforward.

When disputing an item with the bureaus you want to be sure that you have a valid reason and are requesting the correct items to be investigated.

Making sure that you are air tight in your dispute reasoning is important.

You will find that dispute reasons will add validity to your future disputes. If you choose to hire an attorney to pursue legal actions, the letters submitted may be called to be used in court.

Do yourself a favor and make sure you are using real dispute instructions with real reasoning behind them. What is meant by this is that you want to make sure that if you are disputing an account and you do not have solid proof that it is reporting inaccurately or in error then leave some room to be wrong. If you come out and say - THIS ACCOUNT ISN'T MINE, then you is lying and are committing fraud (don't do that).

Sending Your Dispute Letter

When correcting information on your credit report, make sure it reflects with all three CRAs. Even when one or two reports do not show an error appearing on the other, be on the safe side by telling all of them about the error. Do it because the error might be a recent one and has yet to spread to other reports.

Even if you have not received all three reports, send a dispute letter to all three CRAs. Know that you are a consumer, so an error on one report could mean the same error is on other reports. It is not crime disputing with all CRAs. Of course, if you can start the dispute process with one CRA, you will not have much trouble doing with the others. When a CRA cannot find an error, it will respond with a letter informing you about it.

Whether you are using the CRA dispute form or drafting your dispute letter, use only certified mail with return receipt requested. While a CRA hardly claims not to have received your letter, sending certified mail is still best for your correspondence, especially in cases of pressing legal disputes like identity theft.

Call the CRA to know whether your dispute was received. Note that when talking with CRA agents, be careful not to give them the information you do not want to be included on your report.

The following is a list of CRA customer service phone numbers:

☐ Equifax: (800) 685-1111

☐ Experian: (888) 397-3742

☐ TransUnion: (800) 916-8800

As soon as a CRA gets your dispute letter, it notifies you, and then informs you later of the completion of the verification process. You may get a response much sooner than 30 days—it all depends on the number of accounts you are disputing and the speed of at which source creditors give back the verification forms. Still, give it up to 40 days. If you do not get anything after 40 days, know that your dispute was not recognized, so send another one.

What is found in a CRA's Response to a Dispute?

After receiving your corrected reports, carefully read through them. The first or second page should include a paragraph stating the information reinvestigated upon your request, next is a list of affected accounts and the results of the reinvestigation. Here you will see one or more of the three possible outcomes regarding the dispute process:

1. Deleted: Deleted accounts—like they never existed.

2. Verified—No Change: No changes were made. The accounts will continue to report information

3. Update: This could mean one of three things:

I.

Deleted late or past due indications.

II.

After the review of the account by the source creditor, a small adjustment was made, and it does not affect your report.

III.

Along with the forms, the source creditor returns an updated submission on your file (a requirement after every few months) to update your account. In this case, do not be fooled by the "update" notification, and make sure the first issue has been addressed. If not, send a follow-up letter.

Chapter 8
Beginners Step-By-Step Guide for Fixing Credit

Step 1- Get Your Credit Report

This step is crucial; banks and similar credit bureaus, which in turn hold the key to repairing the credit, report all credit information. Most people never consider getting their credit reports until they are trying to repair the credit, but it's always a good idea.

In most cases, there should be no charge for receiving a copy of your credit report; you simply have to request it (usually in writing, in person and accompanied by a copy of your identification). When you are considered a bad creditor for a credit card or loan, the company must indicate which credit bureau reported you as having bad credit, and then you can request a report from that bureau. Credit repair begins with a detailed look at your credit report. Look for any inaccuracies: in some cases, they may be errors in your file, or your credit information may be mistaken for someone else with the same name. Many people are surprised at how often a company reports a late payment in error.

If you find any inaccuracies, you can repair your credit by applying in writing to the credit bureau. If you have any supporting documentation, include it, otherwise simply indicate where the confusion is and request that it be analyzed. This benefits you in two ways: first, if the credit bureau cannot verify the information you are disputing, by default it must be deleted from your file; second, if the bureau does not respond to your request for investigation within 30 days, the disputed information must be deleted.

If it turns out that your bad credit is the result of an error, you should usually go to the credit bureau, that's all you need to do to repair the credit. When you order your credit report, keep in mind that your processors will make the process seem more difficult than it is, since in terms of hours they are not interested in responding to many requests for credit reports.

Step 2- Contact your Bank Agency

Once you went over your credit report and determined that everything is correct, the next step in repairing your credit history is to contact creditors with whom you have delinquent accounts. You should repair these accounts as soon as possible to repair your credit successfully.

In many cases, the creditor's priority is to recover as much of the account receivable as possible. Many people are surprised at how accommodating they can be in terms of organizing a payment process: in many cases, the creditor will eliminate interest or even reduce the bill and return it for immediate payment. If you can't pay immediately, propose a payment plan for the creditor that you can stick to: Creditors will accommodate most payment proposals because, again, your primary interest will be to recover the debt.

Remember that the reason you're doing this is to repair your credit history, so under no circumstances should you commit to a payment plan with your creditors that you won't be able to meet would only end up making problems worse in the future. If a creditor has repeated problems with a client, it is unlikely that there is much trust in the relationship, so they probably won't want to help you. Instead, choose something you can meet and explain your current financial situation to the creditor. By doing this, you can often achieve credit repair quickly.

Step 3- Try and Avoid the Collection Agency

The worst and last step a creditor will take is to sell your outstanding debt to a collection agency. In terms of credit repair, this is the worst thing that can happen because it means that whomever you owed money to consider your chances of recovering it so low that you are willing to lose some of the debt. In most cases, the creditor sells the debt to the collection agency at a large discount, often half the amount owed.

When a debtor sold his loan to a collection agency, he just "canceled" it and created the lowest possible mark on his credit history. If this happens, try and act as soon as possible after being contacted by the collection agent. Before you negotiate with the collection company, talk to your creditor. See if the creditor will remove the "canceled" mark from your credit history. This is something they will do sometimes, in exchange for an immediate payment.

If your creditor is not interested in negotiating payment, you would be in trouble with the collection agent. It can and will happen that the debt collector stays in a very intimidating and threatening position, usually implying that they are willing to take you to trial. The two points to keep in mind is that the collection company bought your debt for less than the amount owed, and you are unlikely to be sued. Your best solution is to offer to make an immediate payment for less than the actual balance of your debt. Most companies will accept this, usually because making a profit on any payment that exceeds 50% of their debt and offering to pay immediately allows them to close their file and work on other issues. When dealing with a collection agent, only offer full payment as a last resort.

Step 4- Apply for a Secured Credit Card

Credit repair can be a slow process, and you may find yourself building a bit of credit backing slowly over a long period of time. A good place to start is with a "secured" credit card. These credit cards are issued by banking agencies that generally target people who have bad credit. Unlike a regular credit card, for which you will no doubt be rejected if you have a bad credit, it is a secured credit; the card usually requires you to give an initial deposit equivalent to the credit limit of the card. That is, you give the company $500 for a card with a credit limit of $500, and they reserve the right to use that deposit against any outstanding balance that remains for too long.

From the issuer's point of view, their bad credit won't matter because they don't take any risk: you'll never owe them more money than you've already given them to start with. From your point of view, secured cards are far from ideal, but if you have bad credit and need to participate in credit repair, you have no choice.

Once you have a secured credit card, use it sparingly but regularly, and are sure to make all your payments on time. By doing this over a long period of time, you will slowly repair your credit history and regain the confidence of creditors who rejected you in the past.

Step 5- Consider a Company that Specializes in Credit Repair

If you find that none of the above works for you in terms of credit repair, consider going to a company that specializes in this type of process. Many of these companies will offer to "clean up your credit record" for a fee. While the services of a credit repair company can be much more helpful, depending on your situation, you must be very careful to avoid scams and read all the fine print that is in most cases.

The basic strategy of most credit repair companies will be to encourage you to claim absolutely everything on your credit report with your credit bureau. The idea is to flood the office with more requests than they can respond to within 30 days, because remember that if the office can't provide documentation for something in your file within 30 days, it must be remote. However, it is questionable how effective this really is, although the office, if it does not document them, must remove items within 30 days, in most cases companies will continue to investigate the claims, and when they finally find the proper documentation, the items will be added again.

Whatever you decide regarding a credit repair company, always remember to go over the documents carefully. Also, note that credit repair companies cannot legally accept payments until services are completed. They are also required to describe all payments and terms clearly.

Chapter 9
Increase your Score +800

Bad credit may make it harder for you to find a Credit card, a flat, or a mortgage. In addition, it can set you on the hook to get rates of interest, which may make credit lines and the loans, which you do get more costly to settle. You might be asking yourself how to maximize your credit rating for those who have credit, described as a FICO score of 669 or under. Bad credit does not need to continue forever, as hopeless because the problem may appear now. There are steps you can take to start increasing your credit rating.

Get a Copy of Your Credit Reports

Before you can Work out how to boost your credit rating, you need to understand what score you are starting from. The first area you must go to boost your credit score is the credit report because of your credit rating based on the data in your credit file. A credit report is a listing of your repayment history, credit administration, and debt. It might also contain information regarding your accounts, which have gone into some other repossessions or bankruptcies and collections. Order copies of your credit reports from each of the three credit agencies to identify. You may receive free copies of your credit reports every 12 months from each of the significant agencies through AnnualCreditReport.

Dispute Credit Report Errors

Under the Fair Credit Reporting Act, you have the right. This right permits you to dispute credit report mistakes by writing to the credit agency, which has to investigate the dispute. Entrance snafus by lenders, identity theft, birthdays, or speeches, or readily interchangeable Social Security numbers, can hurt your credit rating. For Instance, if you possess a record of late payments reported since payments represent 35 % of your credit rating, payment on the record of somebody might have an immediate and dramatic effect on your score. The more quickly you get and dispute errors resolved, the sooner you can begin to raise your credit rating.

Prevent New Credit Card Purchases

New credit card purchases will increase your credit use rate--a %age of your credit card accounts to their credit limitations, which make 30 % of your credit rating up. You can calculate it. The greater your accounts are, the greater your credit use will be, and the greater your credit score might be influenced. It is better to maintain your credit use rate. In other words, you need to keep a balance of no more than $3,000 with a limit of 10,000 on a Credit card. Rather than placing them to decrease the influence to fulfill that goal, pay money for purchases. Prevent the purchase.

Pay off Past-Due Balances

Your payment history makes up 35 % of your credit rating, making it the most crucial determinant of your credit score. The further behind you are in your payments, the more it hurts your credit rating. As soon as you have curbed credit card spending, use the savings to have caught up in your credit card payments until they are billed (the grantor shut off the accounts to future usage) or delivered to a collections service.

Do your best to cover outstanding accounts in total; the bank will then upgrade the account status to "paid in full" that will reveal more favorably on your credit compared to unpaid accounts. Moreover, by continued to take a balance as you pay off an account over the years, you will be subjected to finance fees that are continuing.

Prevent New Credit Card Software

So long as you are in credit correct manner, prevent making any software for credit. When do apply for new credit, the bank will frequently carry out a "hard question," which is an overview of your credit, which shows up in your credit report also affects your credit rating. How many credits reports you the number of inquiries that were challenging along with recently opened you incurred reflect your level of risk so that they make 10 % of your credit rating up.

Leave Accounts Open

It is uncommon that closing a Credit; your credit rating will be improved by Card. In the least, before an account is closed by you, make sure that your credit score won't be negatively affected by it. It is preferable to leave the account open every month and cover down it each. If your card comes with a zero because credit history makes 15 % of your credit rating up, Balance may damage your credit rating. Credit history length variables in the time of accounts, that are recent and your oldest account in addition, to the average age of accounts. The longer you maintain accounts available, the greater your credit rating increases.

Get Your Creditors

They may be the people you want to speak to, but you would be amazed should you call your credit card issuer by the help you could receive. Speak with your lenders if you are having difficulty. Many have temporary till you're able to get back on your feet. They might have the ability to set up a mutually beneficial arrangement if you alert them that you may overlook an upcoming payment. All these courtesies may enable increasing your credit rating and making progress.

Pay off Debt

The amount of debt, which you are carrying as a %age of your credit, represents 30 % of your credit rating, which means you are going to need to begin paying down that debt. If you have a positive cash flow, then meaning you get more than you do owe, think about two procedures for paying

Debt: The debt snowball procedure along with the debt avalanche procedure. Together with the avalanche procedure, you pay the credit card with the APR along with your cash off. Make minimum payments and also utilize any remaining funds. Proceed into the APR card after you pay this card off and replicate it.

You are required by the process each month to make minimum payments. You use any funds to cover down the card with the lowest balance. That one is repaid, apply cash to the card using the lowest Balance, but continue to make payments on the cards. If you owe more than you create, you will want to get creative about finding the cash you need to pay your debt off. By way of example, you can drive to get a ride-sharing sell or service some items on an auction site for money. It will require the Credit and a while, but the freedom rating points you will gain will be well worth it.

Get Expert Help

If you are overwhelmed by your expenditures or Credit situation, you are currently facing bankruptcy or live paycheck to pay, and consumer credit counseling agencies are available to help you. Credit counselors can help you get your financing in order, compile a debt management program, and make a budget. Obviously, the key is to locate a reputable one. Find a credit counseling agency that is trusted via the National Foundation for Credit Counseling. Or, find a credit advisor working with the search quality of this U.S. Trustee Program provided throughout the U.S. Department of Justice. If you are experiencing difficulty making your payments, you could simply consult with a credit card billing invoice to phone.

Be Patient and Persistent

Patience is used to compute your credit rating, but it is something you have to have while you are fixing your credit score. So don't expect it to increase in that period your Credit was not ruined immediately. Continue monitoring your Credit, maintaining your spending in check, and paying for your debts on time every month, and over time, you will find a boost on your credit rating.

Chapter 10
Legal 609 Loopholes and Other Laws

There is a pair of sections in the Fair Credit Reporting Act that you can use to your advantage in cleaning up your own credit report. These are the powerful secret sections of 609 and 611. Section 609 gives you the right to know what is contained within your credit report. Section 611 provides you with the means of disputing the information found in your reports.

Any information that you believe is either incorrect or unverifiable you may dispute.

The burden of proof then falls on the creditor or lender to substantiate this original debt. If they cannot do this, then you will be able to get the charges or debt taken completely off of your credit report. They must send you a copy of the original documents (cashed checks or signed credit applications) in order to substantiate the debt.

The Section 609 is a part of the Fair Credit Reporting Act that deals with your rights to obtain copies of your personal credit reports and related information. This section is often confused with section 611, which governs the rights to dispute a charge or debt that you owe.

Section 609 only deals with your rights to get this information that the credit bureaus have on file, not to change it.

The FCRA includes a great deal of information that gives you the ability to dispute information contained in your credit reports in this section 611. If there is information that you feel is unverifiable or incorrect, you can dispute this information.

The Federal Law and Your Credit

Not many people realize how much the federal government helps people stay protected when it comes to credit cards. On top of this, they also help you when it comes to paying back credit cards and when you find yourself in credit card debt. Sometimes, you will need to search for loopholes within the laws to help you. Other times, the law itself will help you remain protected.

Credit Card Laws

The law states you have to pay your credit card payments. If you don't, they can send your bill to collections or take you to court where the judge will order you to make payments. However, just as there are laws to protect credit card companies and ensure they get their money, there are laws to protect you.

Most of the rights for credit cardholders come from the Credit Card Act of 2009, which is also known as the credit cardholder's Bill of Rights. One of the two main areas this act helps are through transparency, which means you have to be able to understand the terms and due date. The other main area is fairness, which means they can't hike up your interest rates or cause you over-the-limit fees.

The federal law also states that you have every right to dispute a claim. In fact, credit card companies need to make sure they explain to you how to file a claim against them. They will often put up a form with directions on their website and explain it through their customer terms. At the same time, there are steps you need to follow when doing this.

First, you need to contact the number on the back of your credit card. You will then need to speak to a representative who is supposed to help solve your problem. If the problem remains unsolved or you don't feel you were treated fairly, you can then request the name, phone number, and address of the credit card company's regulatory agency. This is the agency above the credit card company that helps make sure that laws are followed and credit card companies treat their customers fairly.

The Fair Credit Billing Act states that you have the right to dispute any charge on your credit card. One of the biggest reasons you need to make sure you keep all your credit card receipts is that they will come in handy if you find something wrong with one of your transactions, whether the amount is more than you signed for or you didn't make the purchase at all. Just like filing a claim, there are certain procedures you need to follow when you are going to dispute a charge.

First, you need to send a letter to the creditor. This letter needs to be sent no later than 60 days from the transaction date. Furthermore, you need to make sure that you send a copy of the bill along with your letter. You want to make sure this is a copy and not the original bill. You need to keep both a copy of the bill and letter for your records. It doesn't matter if you are disputing a transaction or filing a claim; you want to make sure that you have copies of everything.

Second, you need to make sure that all of your information is involved in this letter. For instance, you want to not only state the amount of the transaction, but also give your name, number, and address in the letter. You can do this by placing this information at the beginning of a professional letter or at the end when you sign your name. You also want to include the date of the charge you are disputing and completely explain why you are disputing this charge. Unfortunately, an explanation such as one like you don't want the product anymore is not going to work. You need to have a reason like the company overcharged you, which the bill will show or that you didn't make the purchase.

Third, you want to make sure that the creditor has received your letter. Therefore, it is always best to send it by certified mail as this will provide you with a receipt. Of course, you can always have tracking on the letter, if this is what you prefer.

Once the creditor receives the letter, they have 30 days to send you a response in writing and 90 days to conduct an investigation. There are usually two options which conclude an investigation. The first option is you were not correct, which can mean that you owe more money. If this is the case, the company has the right to request this money within a certain amount of days. They also have the right to force you to pay any related charges. The second option is there was an error on the side of the creditor. In this case, they have to reimburse the amount and forgive any related charges.

Credit Card Act of 2009

The Credit Card Act of 2009 occurred because people were misguided about the terms that credit card companies use. They would state that they didn't understand the terms that were written and no one would explain these terms to them. After politicians listened to thousands of people reporting the same type of misguidance from credit card companies, the federal government decided to pass a law which stated credit card companies had to use more easily understood terms. After former President Obama signed the law into effect on May 22nd of 2009, credit card companies had to change their guidelines and terms so everyone could understand them ("12 consumer protections in the Credit CARD Act", n.d.).

Highlights of the Credit Card Act Of 2009

For most people, direct laws are hard to understand and often lengthy. This can cause people to briefly read the laws or give up because they simply can't understand the language. Therefore, I am going to focus on some of the highlights from the Credit Card Act of 2009.

1. You have the right to opt out

Prior to 2009, credit card customers could not opt out if the credit card company incorporated new terms customers didn't agree with. Now, you have the option to close your account as soon as you don't agree to the new terms of service. Once you close your account, you have to pay off your credit card balance within five years.

2. They are limited with raising your interest

You can't avoid the interest rakes that hike up after you purchase a card. In fact, most credit card companies will increase their interest rates annually. However, there is a limit to how much they can spike your interest rates, at least on the current amount you owe them.

In order for credit card companies to raise your interest on the amount you owe, they have to give you 45 days' notice. On top of this, they can only do it under certain conditions, such as when a promotional offer ends.

3. Due dates and times need to be clear

Some credit card companies used to wait until close to your due date before they sent a monthly bill. This typically would mean that your payment would arrive late to them, which would allow them to charge you a late payment fee. The Credit Card Act of 2009 stopped this trick. Today, credit card companies have to mail your bill at least 21 days before it is due. While you might see this as a problem if you are involved with paperless billing, for many people it helps them save money.

4. Over the limit fees are now set to limits

Prior to 2009, credit card companies could charge you amount much higher than the limit fees, even if you only went a few dollars over the limit. Fortunately, they are not allowed to do this anymore. The act now states that if a customer only goes over $20, they can only charge you $20 at most, even if their over-the-limit fee is $35. This doesn't mean that credit card companies can charge you $100 if you go $100 over. At this point, they will charge you their regular fee for going over the limit.

If you have a credit card account, you have probably noticed a little bar or graph that explains to you how long it will take you to pay off your credit card if making the minimum payment. For example, it might say that if you pay the minimum, it will take you three years to pay off the total amount. They also need to state that if you want to pay off your credit card balance in 24 months, you need to pay a certain amount. These amounts are supposed to include the interest they will charge. Credit card companies have to include this knowledge due to the Credit Card Act of 2009.

5. Credit card companies can no longer target 18-year-olds

Prior to 2009, credit card companies started to target young adults. It seemed that once you turned 18, you would receive an offer from a credit card company. Of course, for many 18 and 19-year-olds, this is exciting because it was supposed to help them pay for their college textbooks or buy groceries. Unfortunately, this caused a lot of college students to fall into credit card debt quickly. Today, credit card companies can no longer approve of anyone who is not 21 years of age.

It is important to mention that there are exceptions when it comes to this. Credit card companies can approve someone between the ages of 18 and 20 if they have a co-signer who is over 21 and have proof of income that will allow them to make regular monthly payments. Another important notice of this part of the Credit Card Act of 2009 is that credit card companies can no longer offer free rewards for applying for a credit card if they are within 1,000 feet of a university campus.

One thing to remember when it comes to credit card and federal regulations is they can change every year. Therefore, it is important to take your time to make sure you are updated on the laws surrounding credit cards, your credit card debt, and your rights as a cardholder.

Chapter 11
Credit Dispute Templates

I t is important to remember that disputing positive items on your credit report is not recommended, even if the information is wrong because it is difficult to get something placed back onto your record once it is removed. Be sure that you truly want something removed from your credit report and know what the effects of doing so will be prior to starting this process.

Letter 1: Affidavit of unknown inquiries

EQUIFAX

P.O. box 740256

ATLANTA GA 30374

My name Is John William; my current address is 6767. W Phillips Road, San Jose, CA 78536, SSN: 454-02-9928, Phone: 415-982-3426, Birthdate: 6-5-1981

I checked my credit reports and noticed some inquiries from companies that I did not give consent to access my credit reports; I am very concerned about all activity going on with my credit reports these days. I immediately demand the removal of these inquiries to avoid any confusion as I DID NOT initiate these inquires or give any form of consent electronically, in person, or over the phone. I am fully aware that without permissible purpose no entity is allowed to pull my credit unless otherwise noted in section 604 of the FCRA.

The following companies did not have permission to request my credit report:

CUDL/FIRST CALIFORNIA ON 6-15-2017

CUDL/NASA FEDERAL CREDIT UNION ON 6-15-2017

LOANME INC 3-14-2016

CBNA on 12-22-2017

I once again demand the removal of these unauthorized inquiries immediately.

(Signature)

THANK YOU

Letter 2: Affidavit of suspicious addresses

1-30-2018

ASHLEY WHITE

2221 N ORANGE AVE APT 199

FRESNO CA 93727

PHONE: 559-312-0997

SSN: 555-59-4444

BIRTHDATE: 4-20-1979

EQUIFAX

P.O. box 740256

ATLANTA GA 30374

To whom it may concern:

I recently checked a copy of my credit report and noticed some addresses reporting that do not belong to me or have been obsolete for an extended period of time. For the safety of my information, I hereby request that the following obsolete addresses be deleted from my credit reports immediately;

4488 N white Ave apt 840 Fresno, CA 93722

4444 W Brown Ave apt 1027 Fresno CA 93722

13330 E Blue Ave Apt 189 Fresno CA 93706

I have provided my identification card and social security card to verify my identity and current address. Please notify any creditors who may be reporting any unauthorized past accounts that are in connection with these mentioned addresses as I have exhausted all of my options with the furnishers.

(Your signature)

This letter is to get a response from the courts to show the credit bureaus that you have evidence that they cannot legally validate the Bankruptcy

Letter 3: Affidavit of James Robert

U.S BANKRUPTCY COURT

700 STEWART STREET 6301

SEATTLE, WA 98101

RE: BANKRUPTCY (164444423TWD SEATTLE, WA)

To whom it may concern:

My Name is JAMES ROBERT my mailing address is 9631 s 2099h CT Kent, WA 99999.

I recently reviewed my credit reports and came upon the above referenced public record. The credit agencies have been contacted and they report in their investigation that you furnished or reported to them that the above matter belongs to me. This act may have violated federal and Washington state privacy laws by submitting such information directly to the credit agencies, Experian, Equifax, and Transunion via mail, phone or fax.

I wish to know if your office violated Washington State and federal privacy laws by providing information on the above referenced matter via phone, fax or mail to Equifax, Experian or TransUnion.

Please respond as I have included a self-addressed envelope,

Thank You (your signature)

Letter 4: Affidavit of Erroneous entry

Dispute letter for bankruptcy to credit bureaus

1-1-18

JAMES LEE

131 S 208TH CT

KENT WA 98031

SSN: 655-88-0000

PHONE: 516-637-5659

BIRTHDATE: 10-29-1985

EXPERIAN

P. O. Box 4500

Allen, TX 75013

RE: BANKRUPTCY (132323993TWD SEATTLE, WA)

To whom it may concern:

My Name is James LEE my mailing address is 131 s 208th CT Kent, WA 98031

I recently disputed the entry of a bankruptcy that shows on my credit report which concluded as a verified entry your bureau. I hereby request your methods of verification, if my request cannot be met, I demand that you delete this entry right away and submit me an updated credit report showing the changes.

Thank You (Your signature)

Letter 5: Affidavit for account validation

First letter you send to the credit bureaus for disputes

1-18-2019

TRANSUNION

P.O. BOX 2000

CHESTER PA 19016

To Whom It May Concern:

My name is John Doe, SSN: 234-76-8989, my current address is 4534. N Folk street Victorville, CA 67378, Phone: 310-672-0929 and I was born on 4-22-1988.

After checking my credit report, I have found a few accounts listed above that I do not recognize. I understand that before any account or information can be furnished to the credit bureaus; all information and all accounts must be 100% accurate, verifiable and properly validated. I am not disputing the existence of this debt, but I am denying that I am the responsible debtor. I am also aware that mistakes happen, I believe these accounts can belong to someone else with a similar name or with my information used without my consent either from the furnisher itself or an individual.

I am demanding physical documents with my signature or any legally binding instruments that can prove my connection to these erroneous entries, Failure to fully verify that these accounts are accurate is a violation of the FCRA and must be removed or it will continue to damage my ability to obtain additional credit from this point forward.

I hereby demand that the accounts listed above be legally validated or be removed from my credit report immediately.

Thank You (Your signature)

Letter 6: Affidavit of request for method verification

Second letter to Credit Bureau if they verified anything

10-22-17

JOSHUA ETHAN

2424 E Dawn Hill way

Merced, CA 93245

SSN: 555-22-3333

Phone: 415-222-9090

Birthdate: 9-29-1987

EQUIFAX

P.O. BOX 740256

ATLANTA GA 30374

To whom it may concern:

I recently submitted a request for investigation on the following accounts which were determined as verified:

Acct Numbers# (XXXXXXX COLLECTION AGENCY A)

(XXXXXXX COLLECTION AGENCY B)

I submitted enough information for you to carry out a reasonable investigation of my dispute, you did not investigate this account or account(s) thoroughly enough as you chose to verify the disputed items.

Under section 611 of the FCRA I hereby request the methods in which you verified these entries. If you cannot provide me with a reasonable reinvestigation and the methods of which you used for verification, please delete these erroneous entries from my credit report. Furthermore, I would like to be presented with all relevant documents pertaining to the disputed entries.

I look forward to resolving this manner

(Your signature)

Letter 7: Affidavit for validation

This is the first letter sent to the collection agency if the account is already on your credit reports

1-22-2017

JAMES DANIEL

13233 ROYAL LANDS

LAS VEGAS NV 89141

SSN: 600-60-0003

BIRTHDATE: 2-18-1991

PHONE: 702-331-3912

EXPERIAN

P. O. BOX 4500

ALLEN, TX 75013

To Whom It May Concern:

After reviewing my credit reports, I noticed this unknown item that you must have furnished in error, I formally deny being responsible for any parts of this debt.

Please send me any and all copies of the original documentation that legally binds me to this account, also including the true ownership of this debt.

This account is unknown to me and I formally ask that your entity cease all reporting of this account to the credit agencies and cease all collection attempts.

ACCOUNT: UNIVERSITY OF PHOENIX (IRN 9042029892)

If you cannot present what I request, I demand you stop reporting this account to the credit bureaus to avoid FCRA and FDCPA violations and cease all contact efforts and debt collection activity.

Please respond in writing within 30 days so we can resolve this matter without any more violations.

Thank you. (Your signature)

Letter 8: Affidavit of method verification

Second letter to collection agency if they verified anything

1-30-2018

JAMES DAVID

1111 N FAIR AVE APT 101

FRESNO CA 93706

PHONE: 559-399-0999

SSN: 555-59-5599

BIRTHDATE: 9-25-1979

EXPERIAN

P. O. BOX 4500

ALLEN, TX 75013

To Whom It May Concern:

I previously disputed this account with your company and it resulted in you verifying this entry. I am once again demanding validation of this debt for the second time as I have yet to receive sufficient documentation that legally shows I am responsible for this matter.

In addition to requesting validation, I am formally requesting your method of verification for these entries that I have previously disputed, please supply me with any documentation you may have on file to aid your stance.

If this entry cannot be validated or if the method of verification cannot be provided to me in a timely manner, I demand that you delete this entry immediately.

Thank you. (Your signature)

Letter 9: Affidavit of fraudulent information

Letter to Credit Bureau for identity theft

10-17-17

HELEN JOHNSON

2525 S CHERRY AVE APT 201

FRESNO, CA 93702

PHONE 559-299-2328

BIRTHDAY 11-30-1990

SOCIAL SECURITY NUMBER 555-89-1111

EQUIFAX CONSUMER

FRAUD DIVISION

P.O. BOX 740256

ATLANTA GA 30374

To whom it may concern:

I am writing this letter to document all of the accounts reported by these furnishers that stem from identity theft. I have read and understand every right I have under section 605B and section 609 of the FCRA. Please block the following accounts that are crippling my consumer reports as I do not recognize, nor am I responsible for, nor have I received any money or goods from the creation of these unknown accounts.

Please refer to Police Report and ID Theft Affidavit attached.

1) CBE GROUP (12323239XXXX)

2) LOBEL FINANCIAL (431XXXX)

Please contact each credit to prevent further charges, activity, or authorizations of any sort regarding my personal information.

Thank you (Your signature)

Letter 10: Affidavit of fraudulent information

Letter to lender or collection agency when reporting fraudulent accounts

10-15-17

TARA BROWN

3421 N ROSE AVE APT 211

OAKLAND CA 93766

PHONE 559-369-9999

BIRTHDAY 9-20-1979

SOCIAL SECURITY NUMBER 584-00-0222

MONTGOMERY WARD

RE Account # 722222XXXX

TRANSUNION

P.O. BOX 2000

CHESTER PA 19016

To whom it may concern:

I have recently reviewed my credit reports and found an account listed that I do not recognize. I am informing you today that you are reporting the above-mentioned account that is a result of identity theft, and continuing to report this entry will be in violation under FACTA rules and regulations.

I have never had this account MONTGOMERY WARD 99986518XXXX, I ask that you to cease all reporting and collection activity surrounding this account which is my right under section 605B of the FCRA, please refer to police report.

I ask that this information be blocked and disregarded from your accounting. Thank you for your time and I will be eagerly waiting for your response.

Thank You (Your signature)

Conclusion

S o far, in the journey of your credit repair, you have been exposed to a series of ideas, concepts, and strategies you need to carry out to make your life better. It is no more news that your credit score affects your life all round, even in ways that you never imagined. It could be a roadblock to opportunities that could change your life forever. At the same time, could be the access point to the good life you have always hoped for. It all depends on the state of your credit. These tricks and tips are tested and trusted measures to keep at the back of your mind as you go through the process of repairing your credit.

This is the most foundational truth that credit repair companies do not want you to realize. It is true that the process involves some technicality and therefore requires some measure of tactics to see through, but this is not to say you cannot do it all by yourself with the right information. In fact, it is highly advisable to personally address your credit issues to keep you informed on the basic areas where you need to pay more attention to your day-to-day transactions. The right place to start is to request your credit report from any of the major credit bureaus and carefully analyze it yourself.

More often than not, using credit cards both for small and big purchases causes trouble for most people. The most common reason is missing payments in a timely manner, which may be due to oversight, financial emergencies, or tight financial state.

While credit repair may be a simple process, it could take most of your time as well as effort. As you have learned from this book, you need to obtain a copy of your credit report. Remember, you have the right to request for your credit history from the concerned credit bureau or reporting agency. You can also download your credit report from the agency's website for a certain fee.

There are three credit reporting agencies from which you can obtain your credit report. These are the Equifax, Experian, and Transunion. You can also check out their websites and download your credit report from each of them.

Once you have a copy of your credit history, examine it thoroughly. It is best if you compare each item with your stubs of payments and spending. For any inaccuracy, mistake, or discrepancy, make sure to contact the concerned credit bureau and request for an investigation on the item in question. Make sure to request the investigation once you have found out about the inaccuracy so that you can take action immediately and proceed to repairing your credit. It is also advisable to establish a timeline once you have requested for an investigation from the credit bureau. Check with the agency again if they fail to respond within your timeline or within 30 days. In the event that the credit agency does not respond within 30 days, request for the removal of the item in question from your credit report. Again, it is your right to have it removed due to noncompliance of the agency.

On the other hand, if there is no inaccuracy in your report and you admit that your bad credit situation is your own doing, you should monitor your finances in a serious way. Make sure to plan your finances. For instance, cut down on unnecessary spending and pay your creditor the full amount due. Most creditors provide their customers with an additional time to pay up debts; however, it would only add up to your expenses if you delay your payment.

When you are dealing with a creditor, it is best to let them know that you are serious about repairing your credit. More often than not, creditors appreciate the effort of their customers in repaying their debts as it saves both time and effort. However, make sure that whatever deal you come up with, you would stick to your word.

The process of credit repair may be a daunting and time-consuming task. However, it is also a circumstance from which you can learn. For instance, you would learn to use your credit wisely once you obtain a good credit rating given that you would not want to go through the entire credit repair process again. You learn how to manage your finances and budget more efficiently than before. You also learn to control your spending urges, specifically those transpiring at the spur of the moment. Finally, you learn how important it is to keep copies of your credit card and payment stubs. Keeping a copy of your stubs could be useful in the future, should you find any discrepancy in your credit report.

The main aim of this book was to educate you on the topic of credit repair and what you must do to fix yours. Regardless of whether you have a low score or a medium one, it is possible for you to fix it just by taking a few right steps in the right direction.

The next step is to request your credit report from the credit bureaus or subscribe to a credit monitoring service, which will be sending you monthly credit reports from all the three main credit bureaus.

Once you have done that, the next step is to go through each credit report ensuring to check or ascertain the accuracy of all entries to ensure that they are correctly stated.

If anything is not stated, as it should, find which strategy could work best for your situation then follow that method to dispute any derogatory items from your credit report. As you do that, don't give up easily; the credit bureaus pry on people like you who give up on their right. Even as you continue disputing derogatory items from your credit report, you need to study the relevant laws to ensure that you can use the law to your benefit even to get more derogatory items removed from your credit report.

Once your credit is repaired, you will feel happy and have a chance to buy a house, a car, secure your future etc. You will also be able to make your family members happy and they will lead a merry life. I hope you have learned something!

Lightning Source UK Ltd.
Milton Keynes UK
UKHW021034271220
375924UK00003B/273